To Abigail
Peace &
Thanks
Rashidah Ismaili
4/92

MISSING IN ACTION

and

PRESUMED
DEAD

Poems by
RASHIDAH ISMAILI

Africa World Press, Inc.
P.O. Box 1892
Trenton, New Jersey 08607

Africa World Press, Inc.

P.O. Box 1892
Trenton, New Jersey 08607

Copyright © 1992 by Rashidah Ismaili
First Printing 1992

Cover Painting by Glen Anoah Kowalski, Titled: "The Silence"

Book design and typesetting by Malcolm Litchfield
This book is composed in Adobe Garamond and ITC Galliard Bold

Library of Congress Catalog Card Number: 91-78394

ISBN: 0-86543-296-1   Cloth
         0-86543-297-X Paper

CONTENTS

Contents

vi

by Sarah Elizabeth Wright

In *Missing In Action and Presumed Dead* Rashidah Ismaili has provided us with an extraordinarily varied experience. Some of her verse compositions are richly hued; others are minimally so—they are direct, undecorative, but loaded with impact. This does not bespeak naivete in matters of verse making; rather, it's opposite.

Ismaili entered this world in Dahomey, Africa, was raised in a household where Fon, Hausa, scholarly Arabic and Yoruba were spoken as part of everyday discourse on a variety of subjects. The maternal grandfather was from Northern Dahomey and her maternal grandmother's family came from Ghana to Dahomey. Her father is Nigerian. She in later years married a man from Nigeria. Linguistic influences do not end in Africa, for when she was nine years old she traveled to France and was placed in private school until she was fifteen, then on to Italy for more schooling and a thorough grounding in the Italian language. Since adulthood she has traveled and studied in other countries and become conversant in German as well as English. Ultimately she traveled to the United States where she obtained her Ph.D. in Psychology.

Perhaps more than language, she thinks, it is the incessant beat of the drums which were a part of her daily life which have informer her verse-making. I must not neglect to recall the habit of making poetry in daily speech which was everywhere present in her African community. So it is from this vast store of influences that her own intuitive sense of verse is born. Therefore, one must be circumspect about applying the word pedestrian in some few instances when word arrangements suggest it. Her poems, while intense and touching on all aspects of life, have a sophistication, a refreshing clarity, and are most certainly appealing. None of the cynicism, hopelessness, and obscurity by which much of our contemporary verse is beset is present here.

We encounter a loss of almost every aspect of human life due to the devastating and brutal slave trade in the first section of the book. Then we come to the wrenching and mystical poem, "Appearances 1": The Strange Ones Came. Their whiteness, their sad and frightened demeanor aroused the sympathy of their Black host. The Blacks adopted them, bore them children, and restored their health. The whiteness was eventually gone and they were saved.

Ismaili goes on to tell of a second coming of the Strange Ones and of how they brought destruction and wrought it upon the innocent Africans who had greeted them with milk and fruit and goats, who fed them and bade them rest. But the second set of Strange Ones destroyed the Africans' homes, their icons and their gods. She tells us that now they wonder why the power of Soboto had not spat upon the non-believers, the non-African. (Soboto is a violent god who kills humans in another's righteous way.) Here she bemoans the loss of African consciousness, so much so that many doubt it ever could have been real.

In the lovely poem "Chez Toi" we see such a gentle and again exceedingly well-mannered heart waiting for a lover to return. While waiting, she knits a new sweater while seated in an old rocking chair. She reviews that his pants are hung and his shirts are folded. Silently, she waits for the day "when barricades are torn, water runs freely, and teachers throw away *misinformation* . . . when freedom sounds and guns are silent . . ." and her lover returns.

A poem in the third section of the book, entitled, *Intimate Secrets* speaks so delicately of love shared secretively with one who by existing rules was called an enemy of her people. In a poem called "Tryst" she says, "Centuries of careful formulation have coined standards of behavior and normal decency is spelled out in manuals of respectability." One can easily grasp the terror she must feel in such a situation and, of course, the compulsion to go on, unapologetic and firmly committed to love's fulfillment.

In Section *En Memoria* or *Urban,* Ismaili speaks best of urban decay—the festering rot of it—the pain-thudding homelessness, the bald insanity of directionlessness in every single movement. She speaks through a woman of the streets who puts it thus: "No wonder God (is) staying in His Grave / This (world) ain't no place for Him."

We see the writer's own anguish in her poem "Help!" The picture she sketches is true for most of us in this financial system who must daily borrow from Peter to pay Paul, and who lives of quiet desperation while working unremittingly.

The fifth and final section, *Resolution* is notable for "The Wanderers." In this poem we meet one starkly emaciated man who is starving, flea-bitten, and cold. He is wandering his way to death. In other poems we encounter those who remain on African soil searching with new and strange equipment, pen and pencil, brush and paint, and formal studies. There are others, new ones who have remained on African soil, who were never enslaved, who have nothing of immediate contact with their captured ancestors except bare and scanty reports in the "empirical studies . . . the comparative literature." We puzzle at the woman who alone and silent in the deep night secretly buries an embryo and returns alone and silent to her community. Ismaili tells us of the virginal girls who are stolen away and cruelly turned into enslaved women for sexual gratification, of the children they bear and the deaths which abort so many of their tender lives, and of the nameless children who live but to whom their mothers dare not speak a word about their past.

We are caught up in the speechless mourning of this living death.

The lament, "O Brado Africano" to the "Blacks of Bahia, Blacks of Yorubaland, Blacks of Brazos in the black nights of Brazil" is striking. We feel the pathos of one seeking acknowledgment of this African heritage in a museum in our Anglo-Saxon world where now his stolen icons are on display under lock and key.

Missing in Action and Presumed Dead is as full of paradoxes as the poet herself. And these paradoxes are often fused to provide truly original insights presented in an arresting and fresh form. This is heroic verse. We use "heroic" in the grand sense of the word as explained by D. H. Melhem in her most significant book, *Heroism in the New Black Poetry,* the University of Kentucky, 1990.

This collection ends with the recognition that, again, we have a chance to "invoke Gods buried beneath pagan Churches where mercy was shut out . . . we who have given much to others (now) give to ourselves our strength. Our best."

ACKNOWLEDGMENT

Bis milali

To all those who listened, offered criticism, I say blessings.

To the sheroes and heroes who are not physically with us I say you are not forgotten.

To those who have paid and are paying supreme sacrifices to ensure a modicum of safety, freedom, I am grateful.

To Amiri and Amina and their Barakas, to Jayne Cortez, Michael Thelwell, I say peace.

To Audre Lourde, my big sister, good health.

To Benita, thanks for typing and re-typing.

To Thelma and James Ravell-Pinto, Amelia Blossom House, Cecil Abrams, Daniel and Selina Kunene and Nuruddin Farrah all who are *missing* from their countries safe and victorious returns.

To Kassahun Checole, my brother and long time friend, colleague, I thank you for your confidence.

My gratitude to Calvin Herton and Charles Sugnet, who took time from their busy schedules to read this manuscript.

Finally, to my big brother Chinua Achebe, lots of smiles.

To Sarah E. Wright for her principled friendship and sisterhood . . . I am blessed.

To Daoud my gift to this world.

May we remember those whose names we never knew.

May they rest easy and inspire us to be the very best we can.

LOVE

"My grandmother used to say
Love is the only permanence we have"

CLANDESTINE

Circuitous, ambulatory,
my feet trace darken streets.
Spurred on by an insatiable need
to be fullfilled, I go down and
around a new place with strange names.

Hugging brick walls I move
wrapped in a full length cape.
No one recognizes me here.
I move clandestine. Free!
No one knows me here.

And then, at the end of the street,
a sharp right turn, second house,
third floor and two knocks.
No one knows me here. I am here.
Arrived. No one knows me here.

You wait, warm and strong. I enter
a limited space. For a brief time.
Arrived! No one knows me here.
Your arms enclose me. I am here.
Arrived! No one, no one knows me
here. Only you and the sad smile
playing around your mouth
is loving. Is familiar.
I am here!

FURTIVE

There was a mirror I remember.
A mirror near a closet where
we secreted our disguises.
In it, I witnessed your back and
its curves. Light foreshadowed.
And, my hands upon your round flesh.
My face darting from peaks of your
shoulders. Oh, how I remember!

And the silent mirror,
shining in dim light.
We dared not shed bright beams
upon the naked contents
of our rooms. Silent eyes
crowded with you and me.
Listening and unremarking to
our words. Glancing under
your armpit I saw my eyes
mirrored by that mirror.
I said something but, as I
recall, it did not speak.
But stood guard watching apart
and a part of us. Our only
witness. Sanctioned because
silence is consent.

TRYST

Phone calling in the middle of the night.
Secret messages left in flower pots.
Signals in old books and, always changing
times. Cryptic codes waiting, decoding
and criss-cross times.

Never did we tire. Never did we tire.
Only in that secret room were we permitted
to admit the strain of devious cavorting.
And yet, it was our legacy. Centuries of
careful formulation has coined standards
and behaviour and normal decency is
spelled out in manuals of respectability.

Yet in that space, we gave pride to ourselves.
And, never did we reproach us either all
the constant attempts to out wit ertswhile
companions fate had decreed us . . . .

SILENCE

In the silence of between seconds ticking
to new moments hides secrets beneath eons
picking each movement clock hands slide
to bring time into focus.

Here, my hands dig brick by brick welled
in notes of histories hidden by hands of
beggars who pawn time against pages of
pious pittance for one moment of review.

Voices begging to be heard find resonance
in red clay cakes of muddied walls pent in
without sunlight. Call names thought to
have been forgotten memories. And yet,
they beg, beg to be heard.

And who will listen to tongues wagging
in the wind? To gossip of wives with
nothing better to do than bend and stretch
under mortar and pestle and, water from wells.

No, better to listen in dark secret hours
hidden and safe, lest someone snatch a brick.
Light a torch. Expose truths buried under
time after time of events sequenced to person
place, thing.

CONFESSIONS

I confess! I confess! I confess it all!
I loved. I lied. I LOVED!
It was not my fault! My heart is an
enemy of my head. I have tried
to synchronize my movements to lessons
taught a thousand times by faithful
and loyal servants of the past.

I confess! I did seek to deceive
those who knew better. I did
contrive to be alone. To sneak!
Yes! Sneak out. Sometimes I ran
out into the streets when all were
asleep. For shame. I confess.
I did crave the stolen moments
in a hidden place. But it was not
my fault.

Love is a body warm and loving. And
I did love warmly. I opened and I gave.
The private secrets of my body opened.
My heart is my enemy. In that room
our self imposed cell, we gave our
courage to each other. To bear those
moments of social deceit.

Yes, I am a traitor because I love without
reserve the body of my enemy. His arms
have held me. I have begged the kiss
of his lips that each time sank me deeper.
But, it was not my fault.

7

I tell you fate has tricked us.
Divine justice of worlds forced
by circumstances to be separate.
And yet, I was river running free.
He swimmer against currents. And now
that flower pots are unturned.

Mirrors are forced to give up even the
privacy of intimacy. And I will say
good bye to the joy of secrets well kept.
Walk away without regrets. Close my heart.
Shut the doors that once flew open and wild.

I confess! I confess that I have loved
and, unashamed I wait. I wait for impatient
times to come. When codes of ethics will be
unnecessary. And then, than I will walk in
daylight to a tiny space and a big mirror
without fear of shame and sign my name, LOVE.

SIN TU AMOR

Now that you have gone.
Now that you have taken
yourself from me,
I look for tell-tale evidence
you used to live here.

Now that you have walked away
my door no longer opens and shuts
my floor no longer creaks
my bed no longer dips.
Even your smell has faded.

Now that you have ceased to call
my ears no longer select
your voice in the din of
modern cacophony.
In this silence I beg God
to come out of hiding
and tell me where is
the proof of love?

CHÉZ TOI

My doors have been shut so long
I am so acquainted with solitude.
Our understanding is such that
silence is all that is required.
We know tonight in *your* house
I will dine and dance alone.

It is by choice I tell you,
that my heart refuses to flutter.
My eyes blind to the sight of
invitations from others.
Your house is well cared for
and waiting in patience.

And I am sitting here
in my old rocking chair
knitting a new sweater
for you. Your pants are hung
and shirts are folded.
They wait and I wait for you.

And when the barricades are torn
and water runs freely;
when teachers throw away
misinformation—then
I shall pull back the
curtains of your kitchen.

And when freedom sounds loud
and guns are silent, my heart
shall open and your house
will be here . . . . . . waiting.
Waiting to receive you.

10

A rose is given to you.
Oh man, I give this rose
open. Red. Wanting.
Wanting. Ahh-h-h . . . .

Each day sun comes to look
upon the earth it warms
and is gladdened by the faintest smiles
that brightens a hungry child
when fed . . . .

11

ALONE

I shall miss your weight,
    your heavy hand holding me fast.
I shall miss your presence
    as I bathe, dress for bed
    in my bed encircling me.
I shall miss your kisses,
    your caresses, your voice
    in my ears.
I shall miss you when you go away.

When you go, my cup of coffee,
crumbs on my table cloth,
ring of wet from my sweat
drip glass; shall be consumed alone
without your comments on the news,
my schedule of postponed dates,
last minute entries or dinner time.

But I shall look inside my memories
and open a flood gate of times
when we were alone. Were together.
And I shall wait patiently for
the moment when you will fly out
of my heart. And I will remove
what I choose. Be content that
you once were here with me.

I have known the sound of wind,
the smell of mangoes ripened and waiting.
And, I have known the sound of rain,
the smell of wetness that chases people
inside their houses waiting—waiting
as the wind raced the rain in greyness,
and green leaves quivered on their limbs.

I have seen lemons yellow in sunlight,
oranges attract bees and young fingers.
I have tasted the tart juice behind trees,
under overgrown bush, under thatched roofs.
I have seen steam rise when rain falls
when hot tin sizzles in the sun.

I have heard cries in the wind
when evening darkens my way,
and, hunger guides my feet.
I have heard sounds made by longing,
have heard stomachs bare against muscles,
have heard a lioness cry at night.
I have listened, waited and heard all.

And yet, you never call to me;
never come to me—never.
I have yet to hear my name in the wind
in the evening. My name is never is mentioned.

And yet, I know you and call you.
I call each syllable of your name.
Loving the sound of you in name
rolling from my lips. These lips
you once touched, once kissed.

13

I have waited at the same place
in the same spot—silently.
I have waited silent and prayerfull,
have called on all the gods,
have called on The God!
Though they, He does not show Face(s)
still I believe. I dare not doubt
Their Existences or I shall turn to stone.

And yet, you are not there. And all,
all is silent. In the evening after evening
the wind whips by, sometimes silent.
Sometimes loud. But always,
you are not blown to me.
Your scent is denied me.

And I, I am here listening.
I listen for the wind to shift,
to turn a new leaf over, to spin
dust against my legs. To make night
eventfull and black and sure.

If
when dawn comes
and you are gone—
do not leave
a note of farewell.
If,
when day is full
and evening comes,
darkening, nearer and
expectant—
you have gone—
do not send word.

Let me find a way to recapture
the rib by rib of your chest,
the special cure of hair,
in a special place.

If
when a new year births
and you are not here,
do not send word
by air, land or sea
If,
when merrimakers
throw pots and pans
together—and
you are not here with me,
do not send coded letters
by couriers and the like.

Let me find a way
to invoke the way
your eyes shine in darkness,
The way your hands feel on my face.
The way your hair curls damp and tight.

And,
in day or night
when you are gone,
just whisper your secret
to the wind . . . .
and I will open my heart
and I will stretch my eyes,
and I will take away the sign
MISSING!

URBANITY

"In houses of strangers
we wander lost and afraid,
cities are places one shouldn't tarry . . ."

He, my man-son seen with dreads
colour streets. Crayonned fingers
dying in his blood soaked shirt.

This sun-shine clouded emblem of
wax / gold digging into cement is
non maleable material, gives back
boot to eye, fists to cuffs.

Him who I never bosomed, entombed
in my heart, weep for eyes bleached,
vital organs counted and checked
for balance.

He who goes dismembered to seek his Maker
meets Him with mangled body. And He,
his Maker will ask me. "What if anything
did you do to warn, to stay hatred boiling
over in otherwise decent fellows?" And I
stand by, head hung, unable to form an
appropriate response.

Shall I say, "Well, it began before I was born?
That's the way things are out here." Will that
suffice pain filled hearts his mother and father
feel? Shall I say, "Forgive them. But do I?"
They kiss night time greetings in safety of time
and distance. Their schizophrenic memory
dichotomises right from space and circumstance.

Each pat of love fondled on their children
makes real the threat of a dark presence

19

they fear. And they breathe easier knowing
they have at least done their duty.

And he, my man-son cries out. And we,
you / me are not able to hear exact words
nor see the very one who raises foot to head,
stick to hand. We are cordonned off by;
"Do not cross!" signs.

Safe, sympathetic and sad we feel each blow.
Impotent in our ability to stop these men
from falling from a state of grace. So
we mourn. We pray for his soul and for
their souls. To collective experiences
of each responds to this situation from
separate perspectives. Seeking a metaphor
to make even this palpable.

But on that day when right will
demand its prominence
what will we say . . .
And to Whom? Shall we be able
to translate the transgressions of the sins of
fathers and mothers, teaching hate as righteous
when cause is deemed justifiable; to balance
the scale
and take the binding cloth from Justice
and beg Her for maternal concern for all.

Ashes and red dust upon grey cement
so much rubble in the wake of death.
You are silent and still.
Your secrets carried with you
falls beneath the onslaught
of modern mechanics.

I see your uncovered self hanging
bare. Blown bit by bit in a breeze
passerbys blame on hay fever sneezes.
That spew phlegmatic mist on your
hush-hush secrets, deep, deep
beneath your pillars.

Oh you who once lived,
once vibrated with life,
echoing with steps of shoes
going / coming, going / coming.

Smelling of perfume and cooking oil,
baby diapers and dog urine. What
do you wish written on the new walls
your demise ushers in? What shall
your epitaph read?

Those secrets, ah, secrets you
carry silently to your grave
will not give notice of those
loves and hates that hid inside
the warmth of your shelter. And
I shall never know the invisible
faces passed on imprinted in

21

red brick debris waiting in a
vacant lot. A gaping hole
that once was a home for some
whose names are long forgot.

To them I say; Rest in PEACE!

Between the squeeze of time to write
and work-work, there are dust filled corners.
And meanwhile, laundry waits in a dryer.
And, there is no cat food left . . . I wonder
at the rate time passes.

When several calls come in each more
urgent than the other; vying for an ear
with daily reportage of killings in
South Africa. I wonder when to plug in
the answering machine.

There is no reasoning of will when ignorance
is supported by greed and power. One tries
to choose between a response falling upon
deaf ears or silence which may convey consent.

Contradictions abound and now, to with-hold taxes
for rent, to stall Con ed for AT&T. To buy a book,
a flower; all lower my banque account.

I shall not travel abroad this year.
My booklist continues to grow.
I shall not take a retreat next month.
My shoes are inadequate for snow.

WANDERERS–1

These are the children of unknowing parents.
They roam up downtown trains.
Hang precarious on escalator rails.
Slide up and down subway poles.
Eat vast quantities of candy.

They are thrown away—discarded songs
singing to a passing breeze no one listens.
What voice will match to words with grace,
problematic manners. Hands not trained to
stay at their sides mouths that form words
of offense. Who will listen to them?

These children with strange looks.
Who keep watch eyes for police
and recognizable others? Who
listens to them? They run in packs
loyal and confused with moment to moment
directionals working. No one,
no one listens to them.

These milk and lost toothbrush mouths,
these snotted noses and stinky-pants,
running up and down, wild automatons.
To whom do they belong?
Who will listen to them?

24

"But if you ask me." She says to no one.
"If you see the way the children going."
she says to anyone.
"No wonder God staying in His Grave.
This ain't no place for Him." She says
scratching under arms.

Her aura is instituted grey walls.
Her movements are limited.
Her eyes clouded, distal.
Her voice conspiratorial.
Her scratching incessant.
This is a woman of the street.

"But," she continues between scratches.
"But, if you ask me, seems like they
could do something 'bout these thiefs.
I mean peoples can't put they things
down a minute for somebody make off with them.
If you ask me, something funny going on."

She shuts her mouth.
Her face is undisturbed.
She stares at nothing.
Her hat askew.
Her hair hidden.
She is slightly amazing.

THEMATIC

"They are missing
   and
presumed dead . . ."

They are missing and presumed dead.
If you see men with rounded heads
and slightly slant-eyes, skins the
colour of night-time without moonshine;
touch them gently. Hold them until I come
to claim them. Marry them. Love them.

When last seen they were wearing KUDOS
around their necks. They are fishermen
and known to ride the wind in early
before dawn dark. Return late in the
evening to boiling pots and ululating.

When last seen they were going towards
the sea. Their fish nets were torn and
strewn upon the ground. If you see them,
tell them we are waiting. Waiting for
their return.

They have been gone a long time.
When last seen they were in the forest
twining threads from cotton trees.
They bear distinguishing marks these men
of strong torsos and fullheads. Upon their
upper cheeks lineage is carved. They belong
to me and have vanished! Disappeared!
Without a trace . . . . Some say they are dead.

Meanwhile:
    Covers slip from your back.
    I search an old battlescar.
    And for now, this universe
    a lava bed of passion rocks.
    Which reminds me
        that
Meanwhile;
    Rocks are hurling across space.
    Pulsate faces of unfamiliarity
    with hands stones are well acquainted
    but, against cheeks a-turned.
    this is something new and bears
    a little similarity to trends
    of olden days
        and
Meanwhile;
    Castles are still in place
    thousands of years later.
    And serfdom seeks new rooms
    to let in unoccupied estates.
    Beg arms to broom, fingers to pen
    to counteract the attack by
    machine to flora and fauna
        and
Meanwhile;
    The earth is silent and wind
    is in the trees. Empty houses
    hang naked and shame is covered by
    a coldness which prevents pedestrians
    from crossing in front of bricked walls

and broken steps
    and
Meanwhile;
    You are hungry and we eat these grapes.
    Spread juice along an armed shadow
    our sheet makes between us.
    We are fed and are content.
        Yet,
Meanwhile:
    Some old man's feet shuffles
    staggering against a soda can
    and he bends to meet it half way.
    They have become partners this
    street chance cans, empty bottles
    and, a double duty plastic bag.
    He is someone's father who got lost
    riding a subway to work. Missed his
    stop. Wandering ever since. Wandering
        and
Meanwhile:
    Mothers are gathering at spot X
    for buses that always return empty
    and nameless bodies in burlap bags
    labelled with country of origin and
    contents, are piled higher and higher
    each day. There is so much food rats
    and vultures take holidays and all the
    sanitation departments close on vacation.
        But,

Meanwhile:

> Bombs split jungle stillness and babies
> look for arms familiar and warm to cover
> their fear and comfort their hunger
>> and

Meanwhile:

> Each pair of eyes lower in morning light.
> Each finger stuck and stinking from night
> upon night without women to warm arthritic
> backs and spotted lungs. Each mouth tells
> the same story. Loneliness is familiar
>> and

Meanwhile:

> In a tent with current T.V. comes to shine
> out the moon. Progress is measured by
> channels and movie houses and the price
> each item costs. It is indeed a better
> time and place to be serving one's life.
> Each rug is an inviolate pallet.
>> But

Meanwhile:

> Street sweepers clean streets.
> They can only clean.
> Vassals are moved daily.
> There is so much territory
> now that heavens and seas
> expand to offer life and
> wealth. There are no limits
> for workers. Speaking of workers,
> that reminds me in olden times. We . . .
>> and,

Meanwhile . . . .

32

Suffice it to say;
>   They were marched along
>   hill and streams.
>   They were in stored warehouses
>   and emptied into ship holds.

Suffice it to say;
>   There were bloodied virgins.
>   Men overboard. Women in labour.
>   Cloth ripped. Gold taken, there
>   is no precious metal for slaves
>   than cuffs of iron and a
>   coffle waiting in tow.

Suffice to say;
>   They were delivered from
>   the bowels of wave whipped-boats
>   shipped from shore to shore. And
>   they cried. They worked. And
>   they gave their arms to machette
>   and cane. Broken backs to cotton.
>   Skins to sunrise and sunset.

Suffice to say;
>   They gave their tongue to new words.
>   Feet to new soil. Sex to strange beds.
>   Wombs to new shades.

When I see hope in new-born eyes
and old ladies in their high head wraps,
even spring green grass stirs my heart to song.
>   And I think

33

what new word can describe the old, old days
when slavery walked the earth unmasked
and chained body to body /

Suffice it to say;
    There was a place where sun shone in
    wild forests and mangroves hid maambas.

Suffice it to say;
    There were people. dark as their earth.
    And, they hunted, farmed and loved.
    They bore children and prayed.
    They wove cloth and mined gold.
    they told stories and danced. And,
    they were captured.

Suffice it to say;
    They suffered and prayed,
    danced and loved; hoped
    and waited.

Suffice it to say;
    It has been long enough. But,
    What
    What if
    What if I
    What if I could tell you
    how sun hot underfoot-sand feels?
    How skin caked with dust and sweet feels.
    How rooms without air, without blankets feels.

34

What
What if
What if I
What if I would say that each day my hate
of slave stench days and colonial days
threaten my stomach bloated and bilous;
threatens your face with my vomit?

What
What if
What if I
What if I put your hand on tension built up
between my shoulders, pent up inside my head
. . .

Would you MOVE???

35

TELL THE HEROES TO WAIT

Each era has its own moments of epoch.
Tell the heroes to wait. Wait for time
to make an event worthy of remembrance.
Making stone from straws, a snake from reeds.
These miracles that griots record in the
labrynith of history. The exact hour is
unimportant. It is the event which begs mercy
to clothe naked soldiers in humanity. Not
their nude arms that render them helpless
but impatience.

Some have waited in darkness, in unlit roads
and hillside hovels for fate to bring prophetic
change. Others have prayed to a distant god
for mercy as a shield and love as an arm
to fight enslaving forces that steal their land
and limb. Still others scoff. They disbelieve
in the permanence of love and dance against tides.

While locust destroyed their crops, the farmers
danced and sang. Their happiness ransomed to gold
and their hopes dashed by holy tablets falling
on their heads. Tell them to bide their time.
To wait for *their* time. The hour of heroic deeds.
And pray. Pray that they will be given divine
strength to make some act valuable to be recorded
and remembered.

EXPECTANT

When will bells peal with joy wedding
lives and births of hope? This
monotonous clang of steel against steel
hammering. Pounding. Shouting . . .
"Not yet. Not yet Uhuru."

I want to return to our waiting bed.
I want to see you still and expectant.
I want to ride the wind and hear your love song.
But, I can't and you can't. The bells clammer;
"Not yet. Not yet Uhuru."

In the cries of grieving mothers,
in lonely jail cells where
uncertainty marks time
slipping moment from moment,
our destiny is honed.

There is death marching in the streets.
I am unable to slow down the beat of
heart felt passion and blood thirst vegence.
Not yet Uhuru!

There is singing in the air and death
rides on the wings of birds frozen
in the sky.
Not yet Uhuru!

Jowls of well fed faces, pinked beneath
an innocent sun, flapping mouths uttering—
"Not yet. Not yet Uhuru."

Time speeds faster in the space of bullet
to body, rapid repeat fire and stones
confronting guns say;
"Not yet. Not yet Uhuru."

War councils in private chambers in this
topsy-turvy era of might and right, impresses
on minds set in their ways. They say:
"Not yet. Not yet Uhuru."

Blackened faces tired yet singing,
keep marching on. Keep praying on.
They say;
"Not yet. Not yet Uhuru."

"The old woman says, 'C-H-E-E-P-S,'
na school boy, wey tin you go say?
You tink say ah be sanza-o?
You sef, you no sabe at all, at all.
Wen you see snake grab chick and
de mudder chick say, 'Lef e o.'
En de snake de gi she back de bohn.
Ah! Me, ah say, uhuru no be deah."

And then I look and see my father
dressed in battle gear. His horse
is mounted. He is in white and purple.
His face is painted and he is guarded
by countless yawa dudus.

"You my faddeh, bullet nah break your heart."
And he, this man. My black skinned father
pulls his gem studdied sword and stands proud.
"Faddeh, you need a shield." He says, "I get
powah from the ancestors. Dey dem come to me
in a dream. Dem say we must fight."
And I stare and stare at this simple man.
His beatuy and bravery no match for
present day warfare of machine and plane.
There are so few gentlemen left.

"Faddeh. Babu, if you don get gun and air planes
you go die. All go die." And this man, this
black skin man says to me under the swaths of
purple wound around his head. "The Old Ones say
this day. This day we go fight. We go win.
They say; 'Not yet. Not yet Uhuru."

I return to my house ashamed and afraid.
My door is locked against my hand. And
as I see dust rise. Hear death sing
in the wing span of planes, I race to join
the old man with black skin and a gem studded
sword. And I say. I say; "Not yet.
Not yet Uhuru."

NOMAD

She has learned to call home
convenient spots where
a cloth can be laid
a body can stretch out
home.

She has come to call a kitchen
any pile that can ignite
and sear a chance bird
or greens offered by kindness
a meal.

She has come to know water
by urine smells and snakes;
mosquitoes and call it
god's blessings.

She has come to call a
distant being a god
because, there are no icons
dependable on two feet.

She has walked because
space did not permit sitting
and, to crawl would have been
sinful since there no rituals
a nomad is obliged to honour.

He is dawn's greetings waking and washing,
prepares for her arrival alone.
His worship is singular in pre-sun silence
when night cool rises to kiss warm lips
of a new day. And he, this early morning man
leaves quickly and quiet. Not even an
indentation of bed and sheet can say how and
where he slept.

His are feet fitted into work shoes
in day light breaking night time dark.
Practised hands swiftly collect keys,
lunch pail, last minute instructions.
Door opens without sound. Outside
too dark for full ground shadow
his figure moves towards guard dogs.
They are soundless, accustomed to
this lone lean body in sunrise.

His means of transport is a metre away.
Dented seat cushion clasp his bottom.
Feet and peddle conspire against dirt
and ditches, tar loss and goats.
Eyes judge time and distance by
break-fast coffee and remains on a bun.
Entrance / gateway, liquid and starch
masticated and down as hand turn wheel
turn corner, round last tree to park.

This is a daddy-never-home-to-fix
bicycles, fish bowls, Paris dolls, radios.
He is an always-at-work father. This

is a sun-up, sun-down movement man;
eat quick, wash fast, quick talk, to bed.

He is a vatal statistic that goes unreported.
His children are accidental proof. Ring and
wife are supportive evidence that she is not
immaculate incarnate. They are twenty years old
household, stable and intact, minimum mortgage
and middle income. He is nearly retired and
learning how to prepare for mid-day talks
with wife and man-voiced boy-look-alike.
Daughter never taught by him learns from
back step ear drop where and how she came
to be. Experiments with volatile substance she
becomes her own data.

They are expected to enjoy these best years
with maximum security and interest free bonds
that do not bind the years of absence by
an undocumented sire.

To the old woman who sits
    night after night smoking
    a bamboo pipe, burning leaves
    to keep away mosquitoes;
    stirring pots and pounding clothes
    in back wood streams . . .
How does one explain bombs?

To the old woman whose eyes
    have seen life and death,
    seasons change and elephants die;
    electricity, running water and
    vanishing feces in water.
To her who still eats with
    two fingers and occasional spoons;
How does one explain bomb?

She has seen star fall to earth.
The old ones painted pictures
on walls of caves. She understands.
She has seen the ravages of desert
sand in winds and dried maize in sun.

But this thing that does not fall
    rather drops. No. Not exactly,
    breaks up in mid-air, and explodes
    with such force all around is
    shakened and bleeds.

There is only the aftermath.
Terror in young eyes.
Broken bodies in rice fields.

And a horde of flies
gluttonous and hungry
feeding on flesh piled
atop earth torn and
fallen house.

She sits aged and wise. Black
against night time. Her hair
is tied against informal times
of proximity. Youths come to her
without ceremony. She has no answers.

Upon her lips words freeze in the
heat of African sun. A coldness comes
to numb a tongue that was quick,
a head that was sure,
a heart that was strong.

She has not learned in the span
of seven plus ten, plus five;
a word that describes death by bombing.

Prisoner X does not exist anymore.
His cell has been cleaned.
No trace of his is left.
Call a witness if you dare.
Dispute if you care, with his guards.
The jailors will tell you.
He is not here is he!

But I tell you, he was here!
Prisoner X was here.
His cough awakened us daily.
A dim glow of smuggled candle light
lulled us to sleep nights.
We knew another day had passed.
We had lived another day.
I tell you, he was here!

Guard P know I do not lie.
He is the one who came each
evening with food for him.
We all saw him spit in his plate.
Guard P is not a tall man.
No distinguishing features,
ordinary. This greying hair.
A gold band on his finger.
Ask him! Ask him! I tell you
he *was* here.!

The others are afraid.
They will not talk.
If you speak to them,
they will not talk.

45

Their time is near and
their bodies ache for
women left waiting in the past.
But I, there is no one
waiting for me. My house
was searched and burned.
No one waits for me.
I have vanished. No one
knows me here. Only him.
Prisoner X. He knew me.
Knew me!

I tell you he was here!
In the dead of night
when silence was broken by snores
of guards and guarded, he read to me.
I who learned to decipher A from B.
You see! Before I could not read.
We would not enter their schools.
I could not read.
I tell you, he was here!

Well, I will write about him.
I am unafraid and my time is
so long. No one waits at home for me.
Death is certain. Let me begin.
Guard P is a pervert.
He deficates on the Bible each night.
His calls to prayer are muffled belches.
He cannot spell. His reports are false.
His name appears as an appendix to
Prisoner X. It was he who made the

statements. Guard P. cannot spell.
I tell you, he was here!

Well, anyway, the night of the blackout
Prisoner X did not write. His cell was dark.
The others said he had magic. He could fly.
On that night I did not see him.
The others said he could fly.
But when dawn came, his cough,
that familiar sound came as
our call to prayer. Guard P
walked with a limp. Sgt. J.S.,
the black one, was absent. Guard P said
he was sick. He knew. Prisoner X knew.
But, he was silent!

Sgt. J.S. could read and write but
could not carry a gun.
could not eat with other guards,
could not reprimand Prisoner A
But Sgt. J.S. was black and the
prisoner was white. Sgt. J.S. could not
go home nights because this is a
restricted zone and he is not from here.
Sgt. J.S. could only beat Prisoner X
because, he too is / was black.

But when the day of the explosion came
and rocks were dislodged,
and the tower fell,
and the current disrupted—

47

Chief Warden P.B. came to inspect.
And all, all were present. But
Prisoner X smiled. He was there.

Chief Warden P.B. walked up and down.
His eyes were piercing and gleamed
in the sun. They fixed themselves
on each man and accused. Each man
stared and stared at his feet. But he,
Prisoner X, he looked at him. Then
Chief Wardent P.B. spoke but Guard P said
he was there when Sgt. J.S. struck him
across his face and Prisoner X had fallen
beneath the blow. Chief Warden P.M. asked
if he had spoken the names. The names of
the others. But Prisoner X smiled and we knew.

We knew he had not!
Guard P assured Chief Warden P.B.
that one more night of Sgt. J.S. and
the prisoner would speak. Chief Warden
P.B. looked at Sgt. J.S. and accused him
of sabotage and threatened imprisonment
if he did not get responses and quick!

That night, that night—we heard it.
We all heard though they, the men
will not talk. Will not speak.
Their time is short and their women
wait hungry and alone. But we,
we heard blow after blow. No cries.

No pleas. First, the sickening sounds
of bone-crush-blows. And then water.
Running water turning red. His blood.
His blood! You see! He did live.
Does death bleed?

Sgt. J.S. cursed and beat. And we,
we cursed and cursed him. Guard P
was home in bed. His wife will swear
to that. She was under his fat belly.
He had nothing to do with it. Guard P
is white and he can hit black and white.
He lives in a restricted zone and
cannot be fetched by night guards /
A note was sent but he cannot read.

Sgt. J.S. yelled and beat. His armpits
ran wet with water and exerted pressure
of blow after blow. He pleaded with Prixoner X
to tell, tell him all. He, Prisoner X
would be spared. Just speak. Give one name.
And then, I swear this is true, Prisoner X
vanished! And in his cell, Sgt. J.S. stood
bloodied. Locked in!

The morning came silently. We were awakened
by a cry of fear. He was not there! He was gone!
The man, Prisoner X vanished. Sgt. J.S.
lay on the floor. He face bloated
and spotted with blood which was not his.
Guard P came in to inspect. Sgt. J.S.
was in the cell. His eyes were gone!

49

His prisoner was gone!
We heard the blows.
We heard the cries.
We listened in disbelief.
"But, I tell you," said Sgt. J.S.
"He was here! He was here!"

The others have all gone back to their areas,
back to their women. I am here alone
in this cell. No one waits for me. And I tell you
he was here. The men said he had magic.

He could fly. He could fly!
Tomorrow I shall look for him.
In the morning I shall strain
to hear his cough call me to prayer.
I shall search the red sky for his face
among the faces that stare at the
scaffold and me. And when I go,
who will be able to say, "He was here!
He lived."

Dedicated to Kassahun Checole

The sun sets slowly on a lonely roof top.
Only sound coming from wind in gaping windows
breaks the dead silence of an empty village.
Without sound children's laughter must be conjured
up, women's voices cannot be heard, nor does the
air ring with cow bells and goats braying; all, all is
quiet. Only the sound of wind in an empty window
breaks the dead, dead silence.

Redden earth turning ashen brown as dusk
descends, descends, descends. Colours of the day
fade in waning hours and darkness falls heavy
without sound. Voices are absent. Houses are still.
No one lives here. They too have vanished.
Vanished and taken the peal of their laughter, salt of
their tears, passions of their hearts . . . Gone. They
are all gone. And it is quiet. Quiet in the village of
silence. Where sometimes dust rises with the wind.
It dances with the wind. Only its whirr breaks the
dead, dead silence.

Past the empty remains of homes emptied,
unpeopled. There is a tree. A baobab, faithful and
consistent tree. Timeless. Hides the secrets of each
pile of rubble fallen upon the darening ground
blaring ghost-like under a full moon. Arms
outstretched and silent. Only an occasional night
bird calling a mate breaks the dead, dead silence.
And all, all is still. Sometimes the wind is afraid to
move. It is so silent. Emptiness is a void that gives

no clue as to what or whom it was who walked.
Who was. In fact, in such quiet there is no evidence
life once was here.

Yet, save for the house top that kept high, refusing
to fall, to yield to dead of sound remains, remains
half fallen. But yet, rains. Surviving. Here. This
house remant of shelter near to a baobab half
covered well and in the centre, a rusting tap. The
handle has given way to time and rust. But, in the
night beneath a full moon, shadows on the still
ground makes image almost real. It is so silent. So
still. No night time sounds. Returned grazing cows.
Chickens on their perches. Goats braying. Nothing!
Not even babies crying, mothers calling bed time.
Nor men walking down to the hills. The hills of
feces they deposit each night. There is no sound at
all. All, all is quiet.

Is this the place, this wasteland?
Buzzard on a baobab, and dust everywhere.
Dust upon the boards. Everywhere there is nothing.
Nothing to suggest former lives. Except, except the
secondary cacti. It comes in the wake of farms.
Though you cannot see a blade of grass, not even
shekeres can be found. The sound of wind in the
cacti is empty. All is quiet. Everywhere there is
nothing.

In this windswept landscape, opulent night under a
full moon; no drums nor dance,

no fires nor food. This is a disappeared village. It is here, here in this desolate place I come. I come calling your name. "Sablou! Sablou!" You do not answer. Your laughing voice is silent as the night. It has been such a long time since I have seen you. And, I am not sure whether the round black dot was on the right or left side of your nose. But, it was there. It was there I tell you. When you smiled your lips spread in joy. And that mark brought a full stop to frowns. Ah Sablou, you were my friend. My friend!

No sound answers me. My voice rings in the night, In the lonely night. Your once-was compound guarded by fences is gone. Gone. It has vanished. It is gone. And gone too is your voice. The voice with a ring of joy and certainty. You have disappeared without a trace. Leaving the memory of your smile, the friendship of your dreams.

The village is quiet. It offers no clue. Children are silent. Gone. All gone. They do not share secret hiding places with me. They have gone too. Taking with them their parents and all the flowers. And you my friend, are missing. You left on a big plane.

Going back to Home. Away from me. There was a revolution and you were radical in your belly laugh strength. You wrote once but, promised, promised to write more later. It had been a long day. So much to do. So very much to do. But you didn't.

You couldn't. The village was a battle zone. It was war time you see. But, you, Sablou, are my backbone. and, I cannot find you.

You are a faded photograph of unfamiliar short hair and pants. You have changed your name to soldier. You have disappeared. Vanished. Vanished without a trace. Were it not for this roof top, secondary cacti; even I might doubt you lifed. Lived. You are missing in action and some presume you dead.

LOST VILLAGE

I have tried to find stones
my land marks that
distinguish even in the distance before
one saw trees flowering.
Someone came and took away my stones.
Even my flowered trees. Gone!
How shall I find my way?

This cluster of compounds a maze of winding alleys
and trees. Cooking areas with big black pots. All, all
are silenced. Silenced. Mortar and pestal no longer
pound. Pound pulp for fufu. It too has been
silenced. Even young girls bending and standing.
Their mouths are closed against smiles not allowed.
How shall I find them?

Each one says they saw them, the trucks.
Big brown. No green. No grey vans.
They came and then stopped. Stopped still.
And men fell out. Out onto the ground.
Each one says they saw them go from house
to house. Heard them call and call
each name. And then. And then they left.
Left. So . . .

I come. Come back to a familiar old place.
I look for an old tree with wide trunk and a
broken branch stub to cup my feet. Like
old days. Days of my youth. I come looking
for my old wicker chest. My shells and feathers.
Rocks and glasses. There is little I remember.

Not this new stove nor four leg bed. I do not
know this place.

But then, they too, the children of village,
are in a new house. They do not know how to
measure their bodies against the length of
a new cot and single blanket. And in the night,
their feet find strange paths to urinals.
Indoors. Without moonlight.

Yet, I do wonder where they are, the ones
who are missing. Vanished! Just like !that!
Once they were in their houses. Eating.
Washing. Loving their mates their children . . .
Then . . . Whoosh! . . . Gone! . . . Just like !that!
Women with warm cheeks and love sore thighs.
Children still feel the throb of bounced bottoms.
They cannot be sure that inside in a bedroom,
a kitchen door, someone waits with a smile.
And yet, they are gone. Gone! . . . Missing . . . .
Just like !that!

Uprooted and displaced,
a mass movement has gone on un-noticed.
I have looked and looked in vain,
in the lost and found sections for words—
But no, none. None are there

On the pages of history,
I have looked in vain to see
a name or place where they
might have distinguished themselves.
Individuality is fairly recent.

But no, nothing. In fact,
I cannot be sure at times,
I have the right names.
Places and events differ from
book to book. Each author
gives a new analysis.

There is a space, a void
where once a river ran
mighty and long. Along
its banks trees and people,
lots of people—with cattle lived.
But now, there is no voice of them
who beat back the desert.
Only painting silent and still
on caves and in the earth;
clay pots and jewels—And then,

Whoosh! Just like that! They are gone.
Gone—They are not mine. Not ours!
We who descend from the silent voices
and nameless faces. O places removed
or forgotten in world historical recordings.

I have read so little of them—I doubt
if there ever was such a place, a people—events.
Maybe it is sorcery! These tales of
flying men and sphinx figures
silhouetted in moonlight.

There is no emptiness. No houses.
Just holes. Deep holes in the ground.
My grandmother told me there used to be
diamonds under layers of this earth.
She said in the Chief's house were figures
in gold and bronze. But, they are gone!
Gone! And dust is thick on shelves with space.
Rumours have it that they have been seen in a Paris

Museum with full dressed guards.
Sound proof carpets. Alarms. And,
it is quiet and still there.
No one speaks above a whisper.
Decorum demands a stance of
two feet from the cases upon cases

in which our icons are held.
And there under lock and key,
special permit allows one to see them.

58

But, I have not seen these wonders
face to face. I cannot write.

No one comes to tutor the anxious pupils left
waiting, waiting. They are so eager. But,
We cannot write. I need to read the small lines
on this white paper. But, there are no signs,

no sounds, no voice announcing his arrival.
The air is silent and still. I cannot read.
I must only believe without knowing.
Without having seen.

But if, the books would open;
and, I could read,
and the chiefs were alive
and water could walk—
then, I too could
mount an elephant.

And enter triumphant
on its back . . .
Walking on the river
to visit my presence
on shy villagers peeping
out from trees and houses . . . .

Proclaiming to all—We are here!
We have lived!!!

APPEARANCE–1

They came—the Strange Ones—
in the night, they came
with skins which whitened in
the night and paled by day.
Each one of them came
slowly and unsure. Yet,
they marched on and on . . .

They came—the Strange Ones
with many cloths on their bodies.
We thought them ghosts
and hid our children
lest they be struck
with loss of colour
as these beings walking
walking in our midst.

They came and opened their mouths.
Strange words fell on our ears.
We moved closer to them—
to see, to touch, to prove
we had not dreamt this.
They were in fact men
with no colour. And we

took them inside our houses
lest the sun come upon them
and melt their bodies.
God never intended for man
to look so. And we gave them
our daughters hoping their line

would be coloured and find favour
with our gods. For they were

amongst us now and we must needs
comfort them. Their children grew
and a new tribe sprung up.
The Strange Ones faded
and became one of us.

They have disappeared into
coloured beings. It all
happened so long ago,
no one remembers what
they used to look like. And then,

and then one day, a group of them—
Strange Ones came. They came mid-day.
They wore less clothes and we went
to them with our fruits,
with goats and milk. They ate.
They slept. And then, and
then they walked in our gardens
and beheld our icons.
Each mouth was held tight.
Each hand tensed.
Each nostril compressed.

And all, all was quiet.
Not even their eyes moved,
but that they gazed and gazed
upon our past. And then,

and then; they moved! All
together—in unison.

They raised their fist against
the heavens. And then, and then
they smote the stones! The stones!
Carved Icons, stones of our past!
Bit by bit they crumbled.

Each one fell beneath blow after blow.
Wahack! A nose! Whack! A head! Lips!
On and on they worked, slaughtering
our gods. And we, we stood still—

afraid to move. Fearing the wrath
of abused idols. But they, the
Strange Ones, were without fear.
And then when they had finished—
all, all lay in broken pieces.

They left our gods bit by bit
on the ground. We looked amazed.
Wondering why, why had not the power
of SOBOTO* spat upon them,
non-believers . . . . . .

And today, amongst some who
have forgot, who look only at
the end results, we hear
words that consign friend and family
with aquiline noses and slits for lips.

The non-African on African soil
has come upon us. And in the dust
that flies on ant hills, and, in dank
dense rain forests, the spirits
of our ancestors roam. They roam without
a voice to call their name nor
stool to house their souls. They
are disappeared. Faded into a blend
of two worlds. Perhaps we shall
never know the real truth. But they,

the Strange Ones are familiar. They
have become friends. Yet still
our icons are without noses, lips and,
in some cases, the entire corpus
is missing. Missing and doubted ever
having been real.

*SOBOTO: violent god who kills humans in someone's way.

DIASPORIC

"Uprooted and displaced
a mass movement
has gone un-noticed"

This is the mystery of a missing people.
When last seen they were walking slow.
Chained and walking slowly to the sea.
The sea. To the sea and in a boat on
the sea. They float. They ride the tide
of the sea. Away they go. Away from me.
From here. If you see them, please,
please say we miss them and want them back.

And who are we who dare dreg up the long
and bitter past? We ask the wind as it
flies in a tree. It plays with a leaf,
dances with a bird. And then. Whoosh!
Just like !that! It has fled. Gone!
Vanished! But we, with our desire to know
and our ears to the ground, hear them.
We hear the cries. Those ungodly cries
in the night.

It is a mystery we are not sure to solve.
There is so much data to collect.
So many variables to consider.
We have read empirical studies,
comparative literature. They tell us . . . .
There once was a place, a people,
a condition . . . . But, we cannot be sure.
It was so long ago and we are new. We have
held pen and paper to hand, brush and paint
to canvas so recently. They are quite
unfamiliar to us. Yet, we try. Try so hard
to believe. To imagine such a time and place
such events did occur. But, we really not sure.
It remains an unsolved mystery.

She went out in the morning to fetch water.
Down, down through a clearing, past a thicket
of bushed trees; to a spring that trickled
cool water over rocks. She filled her calabashe
and turned on her way home. And then, , , , , , ,
Darkness!

There is no memory. No light! Only the fell
of hands and sticks. A piercing pain. Then
nothing . . . .

She sits huddled with other, girls like herself
who are vanished. Each went out of their houses
and were engulfed in a darkness that has no name.
Some are crying. Some are calling. Speaking
in strange tongues. But all, all are displace.
This is not where they belong.
They are vanished!

These are daughters without parents.
Orphans without pity. Bound by a cord.
Chained to each other by shame, pain, fear.
And are lost to their old familiar sights.
These girl children are bewildered.
They have no aunts, no grandparents
to chide their mothers for neglect.
What will become of them?

She who sits with these missing daughters,
does not look nor touch her body which
is not hers anymore. She sits. Stares
and when doors open and she is pulled up.

68

To walk, walk and walk she moves blindly.
Her feet feel the earth turn wet and
wetter still. Her feet feel the cold
gush of wind, salt, the sea.

She is walking in the sea.
Her back to land.
Her face to the sea. But,
she does not turn.
She has little recall.
It is dark and
she has no words
that can define
her new status.
She is missing and presumed . . . dead.

She is arrived and still unspeaking.
There is no face nor blade of grass familiar.
The landscape is void of experience for her.
The cord is cut and she is given to a new woman.
They are black but do not speak the same words.
She is still and alone in a crowded place.
Her body feels older than the youth of her years.
She is a vanished person. Her mother is missing.

She has become accustomed to the feel of sun,
stench and lack of spring cool water on her back
in early morning. Her memory dims and she is
not sure if it is only an incomplete dream;
A stream, rocks, a hut, a mother. She is a
daughter without a woman who speaks her language
and a father who carves wood.

She has become a mother to a child who must not
know her name. A name which she dare not utter.
This child to whom she is mother, who suckles her,
must not learn to call her anything. This child
must not clasp her small hands on her face,
nor look up into her eyes. This baby is an
orphan and this mother cannot give the issue
of her loins an aunt grandmother . . . her very self
to this object she has birthed. They are both
displaced and are bound not by their umbilicals
but the cords that bind them to a Big House.
a hovel, field and whip. Such is the legacy
of a missing person. She might as well die.

And yet she does not. Does not die.
But goes out each day. Gives her back
to the sun. Lies numb and still in the
night. Washes once a week in a tub.
There are no nearby streams and the sea
is so far away. Still, she goes on and on.
From day to day. And, the child she bore
grows bigger. One day she too will disappear
and be presumed dead.

MISSING SONG

For Paul Robeson

He has vanished without a trace.
All evidence of his existence is gone.
His records have been expunged and
he is presumed dead before the moment
of breath leaving body and soul feed,
seeks its final rest.

What can we offer as proof that he was here.
He lived! Shall we say to the deaf; his voice
thundered and soared above hills, drifted to
valleys with the delicacy of a hummingbird
or jasmine petals? These are visual days.
Children demand to be shown. The question
if (the) gods ever existed.
They have never seen them.
They have never heard him.

This man, tall tree trunk walked upon
the heart strings gently plucking, coaxing
each mouth to sing a freedom song. He
was here! He lived! If you do not see him now
nor hear his voice, remember without having
touched the skin of his body. He lived! He
lived!
I tell you . . .
That man could S-I-N-G!!

DIASPORA–2

In the darkness before sunrise
she walks steady and quiet.
Her feet are sure. She carries
a bundle in a blanket.
On her head she carries a basket.
In the before-sunrise-dark
this woman goes towards a woods.

She goes out alone with only a
forked stick. Her gait is
determined and she is sure.
Her gri-gri bag hangs heavy
on her neck. Trees approach
her as she nears. It is silent.
Not even wind is heard.

She slips deep inside the forest.
Rests her basket on the ground.
And all is quiet except for an
occasional night noise. She
takes her hands. Her bare hands
and digs. Digs. Digs. She digs
deep in the black earth. From
her bag. Her gri-gri bag.
She takes something out. And then,
her lips move. Dust falls to the ground.
And she lifts from her basket a wrapped
form; silent. Silent . . . . . .

She covers this thing she buries.
Her gri-gri bag is flat now.
Her basket is empty and light.

73

She gets up quickly and loads
her head. The basket is empty
and light. Its contents are gone.
Gone. Whoosh! Just like !that! Gone!

She returns silent and sure.
The sun is red and rising.
No one sees her as she comes.
No one saw her leave.
There was no trace.
Dew has wetted down dust.
In the silent rise of sun
all traces of her foot prints
have gone! Vanished. Whoosh!
Just like !that! Gone!

letters posted from bright coloured stamp lands
with strange markings tell of missing times and
people . . .

Dear Mother,
I am out of the hospital now.
I am better—all better, they say.
My doctor assures me I shall be fine, just fine.
My nurse tells me all will be well, as she instructs
me in home-after-care.

One day I was fine, just fine.
The next day I was sick.
Someone found me. Saw me
wandering, lost . . . . talking to myself
And then, then they brought me here,
to the hospital. But all is well now.
In on time—I shall be as good as new.
In fact, better than before.

My doctor says my condition is common
compacted grief. They have seen a lot of cases
such as mine. In each case, they have been
successful. Success in restoring their health.

I know now there was no gun
No gun was ever pointed at my head.
The police are my friends and enforcers of
impartial laws. They would not—
not at all, do such a thing.
I know that now.
There was no gun! And yet,
Sometimes mother, even when

75

the doctors told me,
even as they treated me.
I thought, I felt as if there had been
a time before. Before the day
I went for a walk.

Well, anyway, I am better.
Better and coming home.
If I seem strange at first
I may be. There is so much
I can't, don't remember.
But, my doctors have assured me
and my nurse have said so too—
that I am better and will be fine,
just fine.

Dear Friend,
You are the
pregnant pause of peace
that breaks the silence
of winter without flowers.

Your smile is the gift
of sunshine when summer
is a far off dream and
winter whitens my
landscape. The intimacy
of hearts strong enough to
share past secrets and
brave enough to bare
our bosoms to the cold
impersonal stares of
those whose lives have
harbour unfocused anger.

We must needs pronounce
kindness for each other
and best wishes to them
who are needful but
too weak to say . . .
"Hello."

Abandonao
Blacks of Bahia, black Brazil nights.
Blacks of Yorubaland. Blacks of Brazos.
Mi Grido! Mi Grido! Mi Grido!
Back of black Brazil bent under Brazil sun.
Backs of Angola. Black and bent in slave ships.
You are leaving. Leaving me. And I, your Mother
can only cry . . . .

O BRADO AFRICANO!

If I had left you under sheltering arms
of a shade tree, tied up against lions
and such. If I had left you at the end
of the road with molasses dipped in water
with no cloth to cover you,
with no kiss, no slave to ward off Jinns
and mosquitoes; no gri-gri against witches.

If I had let you be suckled by a barren woman,
a snake egg, then, I could stand the pain of
an empty sac. I could bear to miss the weight
of your body tied to my back. But, I have been
abandonned by you!
O Brado Africano! Mi Grido! Mi Grido!

2

Blacks of Bahia, brown favelazos,
where are your fathers?
How strange you look,
silent against the hills,

silent against the sea;
rolling, soaring, separating.
Where, where are they, your fathers?
Where are your fathers?

I have cried my prayers
to Yemaye, Mariama.
This is my plea.
Mi Grido Mariama!
Mi Grido Yemaye!
It has been so long
since I have seen you.
So long that I am not certain
if you still exist. I am not
certain. So long. So very
long ago . . .
Mi Grido! Mi Grido! Mi Grido!

Lost, afraid and abandonned.
Blacks of Bahia. Blacks of Africa.
Mi Grido! Grido! Grido!
O BRADO AFRICANO!

LA CARTE VERTE: SECURITE SOCIAL

I am invisible though brown,
upturned palms with my card,
my green card, my white card
entitles me to queue and question.
My mouth must speak correct
words that will assign me
place and sustenance.

I must not ask why only
respond when spoken to.
I must look ahead not stare;
must not appear thoughtful,
must not inflect answers,
must not seem hopeful.

I must turn the page when told.
Proceed to the next spot marked X.
I must wait patiently.
I understand colour combinations.
Produce careful coded cards
upon request.

I must not forget a dot or dash;
must not leave out a letter or number,
lest the computer is thrown off and
all data need re-entry.

So here is a green one making me legal.
White for work and old age.
Waiting for me to become visible.

80

And yet, I do exist. My hands
are attached to a body whose
legs are varicosed and tired.
This coloured specimen before
your door looks the same

years later, as the ones a long,
long time ago; who stood silent
and receptive to someone who
looked like you. Only he who
looked like you, at least touched
a body. And though it was dark

and she was young, sacred,
and hadn't the right to run
and could not fight—
she who was my eldest ancestor
stands before your eyes in me,

your accuser, And you, you turn
your eyes and dare me to speak.
You raise your fork to food
without invitation to me,
without fear of me.

It is the fruit of my hands
my body you want not me.
I must be invisible.

RESOLUTION

"We exist in a state of readiness."

A man in a big coat
wearing one shoe
walks in darkness,
tears waste baskets
looking, looking.

He speaks to himself.
No one else will listen.
He speaks to himself
No one else comes close.

This man with dirty hands.
with empty eyes,
with loose teeth,
with matted hair begs.

He speaks to himself;
begging fleas to stop,
begging teeth to hold firm,
begging hair to open to his fingers.

He begs God to come out of hiding
under the layers and layers
of one rag over the other,
asking for shoes to fit his feet.

It is cold.
He is tired.

RETURNEES

They come.
They come back.
Our children return . . .
Slowly, they come.
You can barely discern
their heads above grass.
Barely see them in the deep,
deep bush forest . . .
But. And yet, they come!

They come.
They come back.
Our children return.
Showing themselves.
Slowly become visible.
Walking in cautious motions.

They return.
They return looking,
searching amongst
strange village faces
for mothers, fathers;
anyone who might have
known them . . .
known them before
they ran, hid in the bush.

They have returned
after so long. These
children. Tired and weary.
Their eyes are set deep,

86

deep inside their face
and they search for families.

Their families are gone.
But, they have come back.
And as their lips move
to beg, beg their lips
to mouth questions.
Words are unfamiliar
to these returnees.

In the evenings they sit.
They sit before their elders
in the evenings and ask why
they have returned to
empty house. They ask
why they are orphans!

And the elders . . .
What will they say to them?
They look to each other.
The elders seek council
amongst themselves.
They have no easy answers.
Yet, these returnees ask.
Ask for gentle hands, loving laps
to cushion their blistered feet.

The children come.
They come back.
Back from the borders
and bush camps.

And, they look for parents
who are gone!

But,
in my house,
there is a cup,
a bowl.
Here is a mat.
A pair of arms.
Come! Come!
Come to their barren arms.
I am here. Looking.
Looking for a child with
mother missing,
father dead.
And, I will cook for you.
And, I will seek out
the answers to your questions.

Each day
they get up
tired and silent.
Each day
they pull on
dirty pants.
Each day
they rise
tired and weary.
Each day
they drink
a single cup'o.
Each day
they chew
a yesterday biscuit.
Each day
they go out
in morning-chilled air.

And
they go down
down, the road.
And
they go down
down the long road.
And
then they wait
and wait on the road.
And
then they wait
and look,
wait and look.

And
then down,
down, down, the road,
down the road a truck comes.

Each day
they wait
as they did the day before.
Each day
the truck comes down
down the road.
Each day
the men pile
dark and tight.
Each day
they over-crowd
the truck that comes.
Each day
they wait
and go with the truck.

And
the truck
is dust-dark and big.
And
the truck goes down
down, down, down a long road.
And
the truck heads
straight for the border.

And
they go
the men who work.
The tired men
go down,
down in the ground.
And
they see sun slide
as they go down.
And
it is dark
when they come up.
Each day
they repeat
the same scene.
Each day
they move
not think
move.
One foot,
then
the other.
And
on
and
on
and
on . . . . . .

Distant rumbling, earth shaking.
Dust rising in the distance.
And then, and then. They emerge.
Tanks! Trucks! Men in battle gear.
We are under seige. This is, repeat,
Is a State of Emergency!

We hide as we tremble.
Praying to a distant god
tolet this too pass over.
As quickly as rats scurry,
as swift as summer rains,
as light as flies over meat.

They stay. Sitting, no standing.
Poised and armed! Waiting and
coiled. Green maambas spitting.
Venom. Fast repetition. Stones
do not deter their trajectory.
And we are immobile targets.

We are under seige!
Imprisonned and shaking.
Yet, under tunnels dug deep
they come. Our forces.
Hopes of our hearts. Armed
with truth and purpose.
This time we shall not fail!

And each one goes forward!
And as each one falls
another and yet another rises!

92

While under dark safe houses
women gather and stretch their legs
and from each womb another comes.
Thus emerges replacements.

We are in a constant state of war.
Our backs are against the wall.
We doubt the sound of birds
in this air chilled with death,
that they, the birds come dare
fly so close. So close to earth.

To be choked by pellets of tear gas
and other deadly substances. But
still they sing! They sing!
They sing; "Not yet, not yet Uhuru!"
And they, our young. Our Brave and
Tired rise. They rise up from earth.

From trees, and go on and on and on . . .
These un-schooled men who have only
strength of will and love of land;
who cannot write the word *War*

Do not know how to speall FEAR!
Do not know how to read VICTORIA!

They come! They come marching!
And we women, we come too.
Bringing our baskets in hands
water on heads. Li-li-li-li!

These our children made men
by force of war, drink from

our cups. And they take stones
from our baskets and cock their ears.
They hear birds sing. Birds sing
over the ring of bullets. They sing;
"Not yet! Not yet Uhuru!"

And we, their mothers, dig with
our fingers and toes and make
the earth yield. And from
its yield we bring food. Food
for our children-men. And

from the birth houses we hear cries
of pain and new born babes.
They sing, they sing; "Not yet,
Not yet Uhuru". We exist in a
state of readiness. And declare
our own Emergence!

To whom the lotus thanks
    for bloom and smell.
To whom a mangrove bows
    heavy and perfumed, full.
To whom it is whose eyes
    fall upon petals of lotus
    where tongue takes nectar
they are grateful.

To the One who causes skies
    to brighten, darken
    to brighten, darken.
To the One who gives rain
    sun and water and
    snow fish and fowl
    without a single cent
    from me. Neither good
    nor evil wish deters
the Hand who gives these things
we are grateful.

But to them, the children who
    have not seen a lotus
    nor tasted a soft mangoe;
What do we tell them?
They who drink milk from bottle.
    Never having seen the sleek hairs
    flies that hover, never heard
    mooing in evenings, bells k-ling.
Never felt the full teats
    never heard swish-swish;
    never seen milk foam,

95

never held a calabashe on head
only knowing waxed look containers.
Whiteness exchanged for coins, paper—
   sometimes stolen
What do we say?

Dare we say cows give milk?
Can we tell them how they smell;
   the piles and piles of dung,
   the hordes of flies, cow birds
and the women who come in the evening
   when the sun shine has hardened feces
   and carry away the cakes of cow dung
   to burn, to turn in a potters' wheel
   mud for a house; dung for fuel?

And they—will they be repelled?
They might think us barbarous
   after all, they lived so long
   so far removed from the smells
   of fires, cows and rain on grass.
They have never cut their fingers
   on thistles nor woven sleeping mats
   and storage baskets.

To whom do we tell the story
   lest it be forgot?
When they come with books and pen
   we cannot write,
   we cannot read.
What can we say lest they brand us
   illliterates.

We can only point to our totems.
   Explain each colour chosen.
   Each line and mark.
We can say the smoke coiled
   is life's external cycle
   turtles-longevity, grass-hope;
   monkey-protectors, spiders
   prophets, messengers—

But, they have never seen
   wood carvers in the fast,
   in their prayers,
   in their trance;
   being filled with god of all
directing them to a tree.

And they, the carvers make themselves
   pure enough to carve the replica
   of them. These young ones are
   full of doubt and words
They do not know, in between us
   is a chasm.

We cannot swim. They cannot float.
We have no boat. They have no oars.
Only a god can intervene.

We browned and blackened bodies
resound ancient chimes in bones
fleshed with labour sore arms
tire and flounder. Beg time
to wait for breath to catch up
for hear to slow.

We hands and legs to whom is given
a curse of work and a bucket of water
to wash, to drench, to drink. And,
be renewed to work again and again.
To fullfill the prophecy. Beg to see
the god and decree of words and deeds
who contracted an eternal work force.

We wish to know why mercy does not stay
slavers chains, nor lands from colonial
might. We pray for a promise of divine
intervention. Fearing as we bend, stand,
kneel, that this is the one, or ones who hears.

We song and voice in a barren land or
dance and rum hidden deep in bush
cry our long sufferings to the wind.
Our gods have become phantoms. We
doubt if they ever existed. It has been
so long since we have seen them. We thus
roam in an unfriendly world looking for a
kindness which is strong enough to change
the course of our lives.

We run from god to gods. House to field.
A voice, a hand, foot upon ground.
Truly beggars. Our icons are locked up
and guarded from us. We are born and die
never seeing them. Our parents say it was not
always so. But we, their agnostics beg the question
"If they did exist, where are they now?"

We have questions but no answers.
Our parents have not enough faith
to convince us that our hands can
be used for other than toiling for
others. We who have given so much
received so little. Our patience is
tried again and again. Our resolve
falters. Steps fall further behind
our leaders. We question our own
strength and bow again and again
before the weight of gold buried
deep beneath brass.

And now, in spite of our own cowardice,
our chance comes to reinstate icons of old.
Invoke gods buried beneath pagan churches
where mercy was shut out. And, we rise.
We rise to greet the joy of a sun filled day.
We run to embrace browned and blackened arms
of our families. Millions strong. We sing
a mighty war song. We dance in communion!
We gather across the land,
by the river,
in the bush,

behind high rise city dwellers.
We march! We march!

We will once again sing our old songs
of joy. Call our gods to come to us
in a language we understand. And we
who have given to others so much,
give to ourselves our strength.
Our best. And beg our gods to
give us more to give to this world
we make with our own hands.